T0142457

Stamina

A JOURNEY OF RENEWAL
FOR YOUR WEARY SOUL

Shemeca Richard

Copyright © 2022 Shemeca Richard.

All rights reserved. No part of this book may be used or reproduced by any means, graphic, electronic, or mechanical, including photocopying, recording, taping or by any information storage retrieval system without the written permission of the author except in the case of brief quotations embodied in critical articles and reviews.

This book is a work of non-fiction. Unless otherwise noted, the author and the publisher make no explicit guarantees as to the accuracy of the information contained in this book and in some cases, names of people and places have been altered to protect their privacy.

WestBow Press books may be ordered through booksellers or by contacting:

WestBow Press
A Division of Thomas Nelson & Zondervan
1663 Liberty Drive
Bloomington, IN 47403
www.westbowpress.com
844-714-3454

Because of the dynamic nature of the Internet, any web addresses or links contained in this book may have changed since publication and may no longer be valid. The views expressed in this work are solely those of the author and do not necessarily reflect the views of the publisher, and the publisher hereby disclaims any responsibility for them.

Any people depicted in stock imagery provided by Getty Images are models, and such images are being used for illustrative purposes only.
Certain stock imagery © Getty Images.

Scripture quotations marked (NLT) are taken from the Holy Bible, New Living Translation, copyright ©1996, 2004, 2015 by Tyndale House Foundation. Used by permission of Tyndale House Publishers, a Division of Tyndale House Ministries, Carol Stream, Illinois 60188. All rights reserved.

Scripture taken from the New King James Version® Copyright © 1982 by Thomas Nelson. Used by permission. All rights reserved.

Scripture quotations are from the ESV® Bible (The Holy Bible, English Standard Version®), copyright © 2001 by Crossway, a publishing ministry of Good News Publishers. Used by permission. All rights reserved.

Scripture quotations taken from The Holy Bible, New International Version® NIV® Copyright © 1973 1978 1984 2011 by Biblica, Inc. TM. Used by permission. All rights reserved worldwide.

ISBN: 978-1-6642-7554-6 (sc)
ISBN: 978-1-6642-7556-0 (hc)
ISBN: 978-1-6642-7555-3 (e)

Library of Congress Control Number: 2022915164

Print information available on the last page.

WestBow Press rev. date: 08/29/2022

STAMINA

strength to endure or keep going, despite
setbacks, trials, tribulations

Dedication

To my family and friends
Thanks for all the love and support

Contents

Section 4
YOU GOT THIS

Foreword

By Andrea Fluhman

My head. Please make it stop. I am spinning out of control like a terrible roller coaster that just won't stop. On my hands and knees, crawling to the bathroom, I cried out, "Lord, please just make it stop." In March 2020, just as the COVID-19 pandemic began to swoop across the world, my Lord said to me, "Stop my child. Let your body rest. It is okay to not be okay."

I was on the brink of publishing my first book *#wingman*. I had a deadline to meet. My editor was waiting. I was stopped abruptly in my tracks. I lay in bed for three days as the roller coaster of vertigo came to a slow stop. In the months to follow, I went to physical therapy for vestibular rehabilitation. This vertigo episode was so strong I had to train my brain to my new normal.

My life was not the picture-perfect life I had displayed on social media. My Prince Charming had turned into the Beast. My two princesses were struggling emotionally and educationally. And I was just tired. I was tired of holding each piece of the picture delicately in place so no one could see the struggle.

As revealed in Section 1: Chapter 3, therein lies the *lie*. I don't hold all the pieces of the picture together. My Lord and Savior Jesus Christ holds the pieces of the picture in His hands. The pandemic made me rest my body. The pandemic reconnected me to my inner core.

Through this time of reconnection, I was reunited with my friend and sorority sister, Shemeca Richard. Shemeca became my #wingman. Throughout the *#wingman* book launch, Shemeca provided reminders and scripture of the Lord's guidance to find relief, rest, and renewal for my weary soul. Sister, it is okay to not be okay.

It has been my pleasure to know Shemeca Richard since 1999 in a friendship that has gone from sisterhood to partnership in ministry. Since she and

I joined the Zeta Tau Alpha Fraternity, I have watched her grow in her relationship with Christ Jesus to the place where her heart burns with the desire to go deeper and deeper in the knowledge of the beauty of the Lord.

October 2020, with #wingman launched, the time was now for Shemeca to shine her light. Shemeca needed to share her journey and insight into her walk with our Lord. Taking her time from reading devotional books to doing further research of the Lord's word, Shemeca formulated REAP. Reap means "to get a return or result".]Shemeca created the following acronym for REAP: R=Read, E=Engage, A=Apply, P=Pray. She then created a journaling opportunity for her readers to dive further into their feelings. Through REAP, Shemeca served as my #wingman. I've always had a love for Jesus Christ, our Lord. I've been blessed to walk alongside friends and family, traveling in God's perfect timing. When Shemeca asked me to write her Foreword, I was humbled and honored. With a message of standing on God's firm foundation, Shemeca's book *Stamina: A Journey of Renewal for Your Weary Soul* provides a message and a pathway to settle into a rightful position with God, yielding the restlessness into calmness.

The design Shemeca has established in her book encourages you to find your quiet time. Through this book, I discovered a day without my devotional direction is chaos. However, I do not do quiet time out of routine. I encourage you to approach God boldly. Look up and receive.

Sister, it is okay to not be okay. The world teaches us love is conditional. Stay focused. God makes all things, including our failures. Your journey for stamina begins today.

"Let us then approach God's throne of grace with confidence, so that we may receive mercy and find grace to help us in our time of need" (Hebrews 4:16 NIV).

It is in your name we pray, Amen

Andrea Fluhman, M. Ed.
#wingman
www.andreafluhmanbooks.com

Preface

About eight years ago, I was laid off from a job that I loved. During this time, God told me to write a book. I laughed. I said, "Seriously God. I am a single mother and I need to find a job. Not sure where I would find the time to write a book." The idea of writing a book would not go away. I started a blog website instead. I also started writing devotions for another website, LaneofRoses.com. I then told God, "Here you go. This is about all I can do."

Then life happened. I became inconsistent with the blog. The Holy Spirit continued to nudge me to write the book. I started taking some classes, thinking that would subdue the nudge. Life continued to happen. Then COVID happened. As a mental health professional, I started to realize that just about everyone was feeling weary and/or anxious. That is when I understood the assignment. I understood the assignment and call to write a book—this book. The passion and desire grew deeper and deeper. I was determined more than anything to get this book written. I was determined to get this book into your hands.

Life continued to happen. If I only had the space and time, I would tell you everything that arose while writing this book. There were many times that I was more than weary. With lots of tears and prayer, I depended on God and encouraged myself as I wrote this book for you.

My life has been anything but easy. I grew up in a small town in Louisiana. I was bullied all through high school. I had low self-esteem and was not sure where I fit in or if I fit in. I moved from Louisiana to Texas the day after high school graduation with no intentions of looking back.

I studied psychology because I really needed to know why people act the way they do, especially my family and those around me. I thought this was a personal challenge that I needed to tackle. Little did I know that I was walking right into my purpose. I graduated from West Texas A&M

University with a BA in Psychology. I was in love with helping others. I just knew that I had to change the world. I started working for Children's Protective Services, as I felt that I could relate to the children who were experiencing trauma. I wanted to save as many children as possible. I was a twenty-three-year-old wanting to make a difference in the world. Years later, I moved to the Houston area. I obtained my MA in Behavioral Sciences. Now I was truly ready to save and change lives.

If only life went the way we planned, right? The trials of life came and knocked me off me feet. I was hit with disappointments and unanswered prayers. I was bruised by life and many disappointments. Many times, I was left feeling desperate and discouraged. I experienced many seasons of sorrow and struggles. But through it all, I learned that my struggles were used to bring me closer to God. Struggles and sorrow can be great life experiences if we allow God to work through us.

I know the pain of rejection. I know the agony of wanting to be loved and accepted. In my life there have been so many *Where have I gone wrong? When is it my turn?* moments.

I know that it seems tough—wait—I know that it is tough. I understand the pain and feeling of abandonment. But I invite you to stay focused on Jesus. Keep your eyes fixed above on Him. Seek Jesus continually. Begin each day asking Him for guidance, peace, and clarity.

I fought so many battles of weariness and anxiousness. Through every battle, struggle, and sorrow, Jesus was there. I learned to lay all my cares at His feet. I understood the importance of lamenting. I learned that it is okay to not be okay. I realized that Jesus is with me in my struggles. I wrote this book to encourage you. I still battle and struggle with weariness at times, but I lean on Jesus. Reading this devotional will help you learn to lean on Jesus and lay your burdens of weariness at His feet.

Introduction

Hey sister,

Are you feeling weary? Stressed out? Burned out? Overwhelmed? Physically and mentally exhausted? Emotionally drained? Frustrated? Empty? Discouraged? Do you feel like a ton of bricks is on your shoulders? Are you feeling that you can't break free, no matter what you try? My dear sister, I hear you. I see you. I am you.

Every day is filled with uncertainty. Each day presents responsibilities and challenges. You take your responsibilities seriously. Those responsibilities come with burdens—heavy burdens. You wear your burdens proudly and quietly until you cannot wear them anymore. Now you are feeling stuck and need some relief. You need renewed strength. You now need hope. You need encouragement. I understand your frustrations and feelings of discouragement and weariness. I wrote this book just for you.

You have dreams, hopes, and goals that you want to accomplish, but the burdens of life keep getting in the way. This devotional book will provide you with the techniques (power) needed to find the strength, renewed hope, and stamina that you are desperately seeking for your weary soul.

My desire is to take you on a journey of discovering how to trust Jesus to lead and guide you so that you can maintain the endurance and stamina to keep moving forward despite life's challenges.

During this journey you will

- Lay down and release your burdens at Jesus's feet through lamentation (Section 1);
- Embrace God's promises through understanding His character (Section 2);

- Revitalize your mind, soul, and spirit (Section 3); and
- Seize the opportunity to renew your hope by tapping into inner strength that only God can provide (Section 4).

I am sharing these devotions because I have felt distressed and overwhelmed most of my life. My life was chaotic. My soul was weary. I experienced divorce, single parenting, job loss, and health issues. During each of these hardships, I felt that I was not loved by God or by anyone. I felt that the weary and chaotic life was one that I was intended to live. It seemed like each time I made any progress, I would get pushed back ten steps. Through it all, I learned to take all my worries, cares, and burdens to Jesus. Jesus has been my friend, my healer, my counselor, and my provider. I laid my burdens at Jesus's feet and depended on him. He has never left me alone. I accepted who I am in His eyes. I accepted that Jesus loves me. I accepted that Jesus bestows compassion, grace, and mercy on me.

No matter the circumstance or situation, be encouraged. Know that Jesus renews, heals, and strengthens. There is nothing—no situation or circumstance—that is too hard for God (Luke 1:37). There is no situation or circumstance that He cannot handle. Renewed hope and stamina are available through Jesus. Jesus wants you to take your burdens to Him. He will renew your strength each day if you allow Him. He gives you vigor and vitality to keep running toward your purpose.

You will embark on a journey where you will gain relief, rest, and renewal for your weary soul. I desire for you to have the stamina to endure every hardship, test, and trial that life throws your way.

I know that you have been praying and wondering when things will get better. They will get better. Don't give up. Don't' stop believing, trusting, and putting in the work. Keep up the stamina to endure life's challenges.

End of Chapter Journaling

At the end of each chapter, you will have the opportunity to REAP. Reap means "to get a return or result."

R=Read, E=Engage, A=Apply, P=Pray

A scripture is provided so you can reflect on the devotion you just read.

Respond to Scripture: This is the familiarize yourself with the scripture stage.

- Read/write out the verse.
- Read the verses that precede and follow this one to get a better understanding of the scripture.

Engage: This is the meditation stage.

- What words stand out to you the most?
- What commands do you see?
- What principles do you see?

Apply: This is preparation for real-life application.

- How can you apply the scripture to your life?
- How can you apply this scripture/devotion to your daily walk with God?

Pray: Talk to God about what you learned.

- Have a conversation with God about what you learned. Ask Him to guide you by showing you how to apply this verse to your life.
- Ask God to show you His truths and promises.
- Write out what God is speaking to you. Live it out by *standing* on His *promises*.

The butterflies

There are butterflies at the top of each page. The butterflies represent endurance and transformation. They are friendly reminders of your goal of stamina at the end of this journey.

Section 1

RELEASE THE BURDEN

INTRODUCTION

Come to Me, all you who labor and are heavy laden, and I will give you rest. Take My yoke upon you and learn from Me, for I am gentle and lowly in heart, and you will find rest for your souls.
—MATTHEW 11:28-29 NIV

My dear sister,

Your journey begins with a release. It is time to let go of the heavy burdens, worry, stress, and uncontrollable circumstances. I love how Jesus says, "Come to Me." This is an invitation. Jesus is telling us to bring our burdens, responsibilities, grievances, cares, concerns, sorrows, afflictions, and anxieties to Him. In return, He will give you rest and relief. Yes, my sister, it is that simple. There is no trickery involved—just rest for your weary soul.

This section helps you to accept and process the raw emotions of pain, suffering, hardship, worry, anxiety, and sorrow. Take heart and be assured that you can lay all your cares at Jesus's feet, because He cares for you.

Day 1

IT IS OKAY TO NOT BE OKAY

Be gracious to me, O Lord, for I am in distress; my eye is wasted from grief; my soul and my body also. For my life is spent with sorrow, and my years with sighing; my strength fails because of my iniquity, and my bones waste away.
—PSALM 31:9–10 ESV

Your soul is tired, weary, fatigued, and exhausted. Most times when we feel weary, we feel that there is no way out. If anyone knows about the weary soul, it is David.

David was a man after God's own heart. Yet, David was human, just like you and me. David was in the cave fighting for his life because King Saul wanted to kill him. David felt worn out, weary, stressed, and distressed. Here in Psalm 13, you can see that David's heart was filled with anguish and sorrow. He asked God to answer his pleas. He was desperate. David needed and wanted God to rescue him. He felt deep sorrow.

> How long, LORD? Will you forget me forever? How long will you hide your face from me? How long must I wrestle with my thoughts and day after day have sorrow in my heart? How long will my enemy triumph over me? Look on me and answer, LORD my God. Give light to my eyes, or I will sleep in death, and my enemy will say, "I have overcome him," and my foes will rejoice when I fall. But I trust in your unfailing love; my heart rejoices in your

> salvation I will sing the Lord's praise, for he has been good to me. (Psalm 13 NIV)

Life will happen. Like David, your life can be chaotic, painful, and messy at times. There are disappointments, hurts, and hardships that are exhausting and draining. The pain is raw, brutal, and overwhelming. Most times, it feels that the pain will never end. It is okay to experience these feelings. It is okay to not be okay. You have permission to acknowledge your sorrows, weariness, exhaustion, and despair. The key is not to get stuck in those feelings. In Psalm 13 verses 5 and 6, David speaks of his confidence in God's faithful love. Life is full of twists, turns, and detours.

Through it all, be confident that God is on your side, and everything will be okay. It may not be okay right now. It may hurt right now, but it will be okay in the end.

Stamina to REAP

Respond to Scripture: This is the familiarize yourself with the scripture stage.

- Read/write the verse.
- Read the verses that precede and follow this one to get a better understanding.

Be gracious to me, O Lord, for I am in distress; my eye is wasted from grief; my soul and my body also. For my life is spent with sorrow, and my years with sighing; my strength fails because of my iniquity, and my bones waste away. (Psalm 31:9–10 ESV)

Engage: This is the meditation stage.

- What words stand out to you the most?
- What commands do you see?
- What principles do you see?

Apply: This is preparation for real-life application.

- ➲ How can you apply the scripture to your life?
- ➲ How can you apply this scripture/devotion to your daily walk with God?

Pray: Talk to God about what you learned.

- ➲ Have a conversation with God about what you learned. Ask Him to guide you by showing you how to apply this verse to your life.
- ➲ Ask God to show you His truths and promises.
- ➲ Write out what God is speaking to you. Live it out by *standing* on His *promises.*

Journal other thoughts/insight

Day 2

CRY OUT

My God, my God, why have you forsaken me? Why are you so far from saving me, from the words of my groaning? O my God, I cry by day, but you do not answer, and by night, but I find no rest.
—PSALM 22:1–2 ESV

Falling to the floor in despair, all I could do was cry. My heart was broken. At this point, I had no words—only thoughts. My thoughts were not too good. I thought, *Why is life so hard? Why does no one care about me? Why is everything falling apart? Why is nothing going right? Where are you God? Do you not hear or see me? God, why have you forsaken me? Why have you allowed this to happen to me?* These are all thoughts that continued to repeat over and over in my head.

I learned about lamenting when I read the book *Dark Clouds, Deep Mercy: Discovering the Grace of Lament*. To *lament* means "to cry out while expressing deep grief and sorrow."[1] Sorrow is "distress caused by disappointment, loss, suffering, and hardships."[2] One can lament over the loss of a person or something that was especially important to him or her. After reading this book, I realized that I was lamenting unintentionally. I was lamenting over the loss of that marriage. I was lamenting over the loss of that job. I was lamenting over that financial setback. I realized that God gives us permission to lament, so I decided to start lamenting intentionally.

---

[1] Mark Vroegop, *Dark Clouds, Deep Mercy Discovering the Grace of Lament* (Wheaton, IL: Crossway, 2019), 28.

[2] "Sorrow," s.v. Dictionary.com, accessed June 30, 2022, http://dictionary.reference.com/browse/sorrow.

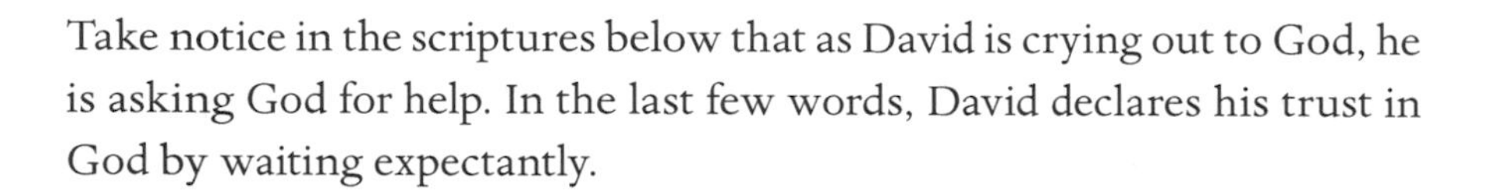

There are four elements of lamentation:

- Speaking to God about the concern/grievance;
- Describing the concern/grievance;
- Asking God for His help; and
- Declaring your trust in God.[3]

Take notice in the scriptures below that as David is crying out to God, he is asking God for help. In the last few words, David declares his trust in God by waiting expectantly.

> Listen to my words, Lord, consider my lament. Hear my cry for help, my King and my God, for to you I pray. In the morning, Lord, you hear my voice; in the morning I lay my requests before you and wait expectantly.—Psalm 5:1–3 NIV

God wants us to pour out our hearts to him. He understands our pain. When we lament and cry out to God, we release sorrow and pain. The word *morning* in verse three represents renewed hope each day. With those feelings of pain and sorrow, continue to cry out to God each day, as needed, with a sense of renewed hope. Continue to trust and believe that God will answer your cries.

---

[3] Vroegop, *Dark Clouds*, 29.

Stamina to REAP

Respond to Scripture: This is the familiarize yourself with the scripture stage.

- Read/write the verse.
- Read the verses that precede and follow this one to get a better understanding.

My God, my God, why have you forsaken me? Why are you so far from saving me, from the words of my groaning? O my God, I cry by day, but you do not answer, and by night, but I find no rest. (Psalm 22:1–2 ESV)

Engage: This is the meditation stage.

- What words stand out to you the most?
- What commands do you see?
- What principles do you see?

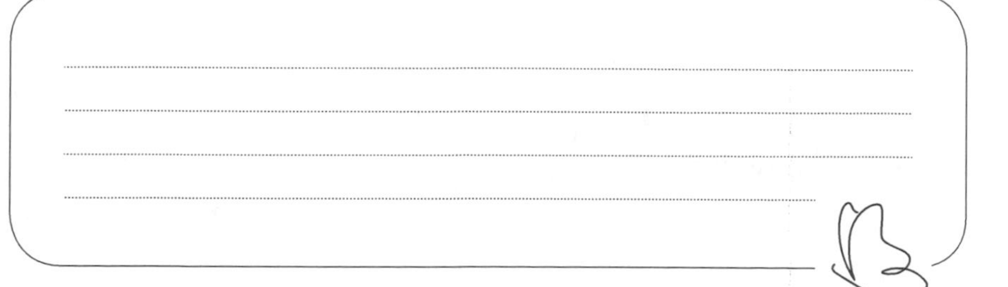

Apply: This is preparation for real-life application.

- How can you apply the scripture to your life?
- How can you apply this scripture/devotion to your daily walk with God?

Pray: Talk to God about what you learned.

- Have a conversation with God about what you learned. Ask Him to guide you by showing you how to apply this verse to your life.
- Ask God to show you His truths and promises.
- Write out what God is speaking to you. Live it out by *standing* on His *promises.*

Journal other thoughts/insight

Day 3

LAY IT ALL DOWN

"Come to me, all you who are weary and burdened, and I will give you rest. Take my yoke upon you and learn from me, for I am gentle and humble in heart, and you will find rest for your souls."
—MATTHEW 11:28–29 NIV

As I sat during my quiet time, a waterfall of tears flowed down my face. I asked God, "Why has my life turned out like this? What did I do to deserve this?" My soul was overwhelmed. I was continuing to deal with hardships, heartache, and pain. There was a sharp, tense feeling in my heart. My breathing was shallow. It was in this moment that Jesus reminded me to give it all to Him. Jesus reminded me that He understands what it feels like to be overwhelmed by carrying burdens. Trust me, Jesus knows burdens. Is there a burden greater than dying to save sinful humankind? Jesus became overwhelmed with the burden of dying for us sinners. He became so overwhelmed that he asked God to remove the burden from Him,

> saying, "Father, if you are willing, remove this cup from me. Nevertheless, not my will, but yours, be done." (Luke 22:42 ESV)

My sister, it is not your responsibility to carry your burdens, cares, and concerns. Carrying the dead weight, hindrances, and grievances leads to stress, depression, and oppression. The stress, depression, and oppression lead to physical ailments such as headaches, stomachaches, fatigue, lack of energy, mood swings, lack of sleep, crying spells, and lack of motivation.

Sweet sister, do it now. Lay down your cares. It is time to be open and transparent with Jesus. After all, He knows what you are going through. Jesus is waiting for you. Go to your private place and pray, wail, and cry out. Tell Jesus how hard it has been for you to carry all this weight. And then do it. Drop it! Drop all the weight and burdens. Do not hold anything back. Jesus will take it from there. He will give you rest and relief so that you can keep moving forward.

Jesus invites you to come to Him. He promises to give you rest from the weariness of your burdens and the daily burnout.

Stamina to REAP

Respond to Scripture: This is the familiarize yourself with the scripture stage.

- Read/write the verse.
- Read the verses that precede and follow this one to get a better understanding.

Come to me, all you who are weary and burdened, and I will give you rest. Take my yoke upon you and learn from me, for I am gentle and humble in heart, and you will find rest for your souls. (Matthew 11:28–29 NIV)

Engage: This is the meditation stage.

- What words stand out to you the most?
- What commands do you see?
- What principles do you see?

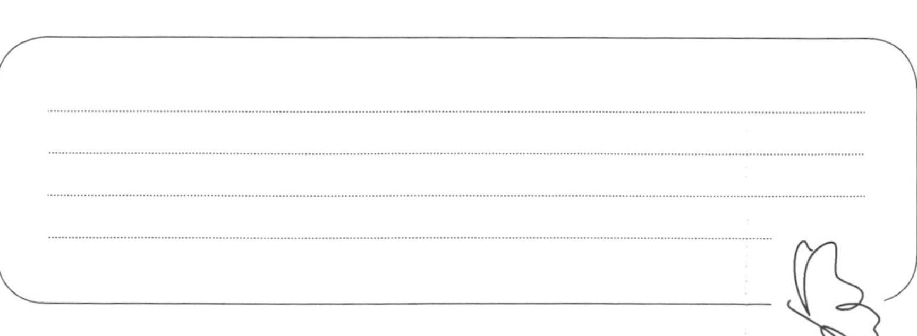

Apply: This is preparation for real-life application.

- How can you apply the scripture to your life?
- How can you apply this scripture/devotion to your daily walk with God?

Pray: Talk to God about what you learned.

- Have a conversation with God about what you learned. Ask Him to guide you by showing you how to apply this verse to your life.
- Ask God to show you His truths and promises.
- Write out what God is speaking to you. Live it out by *standing* on His *promises*.

Journal other thoughts/insights

Day 4

ENCOURAGED SOUL

The Lord is close to the brokenhearted and saves those who are crushed in spirit.
—PSALM 34:18 NIV

My sweet sister, you did it! You cried out and laid your burdens and concerns down at Jesus's feet. This probably was not easy. You are so brave for doing so. You are so courageous for baring your true, naked, and raw emotions. It takes courage to bear all your worries, concerns, and weaknesses. Jesus was there with you the entire time. He knows all and sees all. Jesus knows all about everything that you have been holding on to. He knows about your crushed spirit, brokenness, and hurt. Jesus is with you through it all. He will save you through His mercy, grace, and compassion. Jesus is passionate about you.

Jesus sees each and every tear that falls from your eyes. My favorite imagery of this is from the movie *The Shack*. Mack, the main character, has met God, Jesus, and the Holy Spirit. When Mack cries, the Holy Spirit removes a little bottle and catches Mack's tears.[4] This is what I imagine being done. I think about Jesus catching all my tears and putting them in a bottle (Psalm 56:8 ESV). I am encouraged that Jesus shows compassion for my cares and concerns.

My dear sister, now is the time to start being encouraged. God will never leave you or forsake you. It may sound cliché, but it is true. It is this simple promise that gives me peace in some of the hardest moments of my life. It is so calming to repeat this verse over and over again in my head or aloud. It encourages and gently reminds me that God is with me.

---

[4] *The Shack*, directed by Stuart Hazeldine (Lionsgate, 2017).

I want to encourage you as we continue through this journey. When you feel alone or that no one cares or understands, remember that Jesus does. He will never leave you alone.

> The Lord himself goes before you and will be with you; he will never leave you nor forsake you. Do not be afraid; do not be discouraged. (Deuteronomy 31:8 NIV)

Jesus knows about every tear, every sigh, every heartache, and every moment of loneliness. He knows. Jesus sees and knows everything about you.

In this moment, start feeling encouraged. In this moment, start realizing that Jesus is ready to restore, renew, and strengthen your crushed spirit and brokenness. Find encouragement in knowing that Jesus is here to help you pick up the broken pieces.

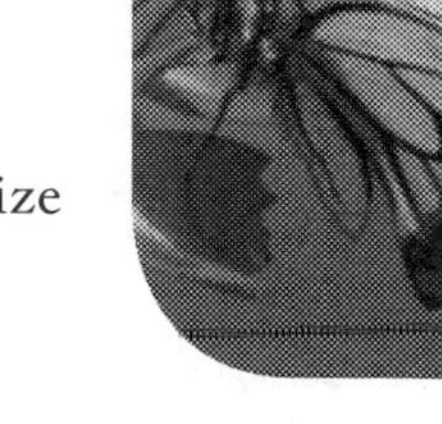

Stamina to REAP

Respond to Scripture: This is the familiarize yourself with the scripture stage.

- Read/write the verse.
- Read the verses that precede and follow this one to get a better understanding.

The Lord is close to the brokenhearted and saves those who are crushed in spirit. (Psalm 34:18 NIV)

Engage: This is the meditation stage.

- What words stand out to you the most?
- What commands do you see?
- What principles do you see?

Apply: This is preparation for real-life application.

- How can you apply the scripture to your life?
- How can you apply this scripture/devotion to your daily walk with God?

Pray: Talk to God about what you learned.

- Have a conversation with God about what you learned. Ask Him to guide you by showing you how to apply this verse to your life.
- Ask God to show you His truths and promises.
- Write out what God is speaking to you. Live it out by *standing* on His *promises.*

Journal other thoughts/insights

Day 5
HEARTFELT COMFORT

Though you have made me see troubles, many and bitter, you will restore my life again; from the depths of the earth you will again bring me up. You will increase my honor and comfort me once more.
—PSALM 71:20–21 NIV

Safety and security are what come to mind when I think about comfort. Comfort is that warm, tingly feeling that helps you feel reassured. Comfort is needed when we are feeling weak, heartbroken, and abandoned. Jesus is a comforter. He can and will provide comfort for us as we navigate trials, tribulations, weariness, and brokenness. Each trial, circumstance, and situation you face may require a unique style of comfort.

Here are a few different styles of comfort.

Peace is the sense of feeling fearless. When you are at peace, you feel freedom from threat. Jesus provides us with a sweet peace that goes beyond our understanding (Philippians 4:7 ESV).

Clarity is the sense of understanding. Wisdom and clarity are gained through the Holy Spirit (James 1:5 NIV).

Closeness is the feeling that Jesus is near. Intimacy is felt through closeness. This closeness feels as if Jesus is wrapping His loving arms around you (Psalm 91:4 NLT).

I need peace, clarity, and intimacy in many different circumstances and situations. Jesus provides that comfort to me each time I need it. Each one of those concerns, worries, burdens, struggles, and hardships is now at the feet of Jesus. Now that you have laid down all your burdens at His feet, accept the peace, clarity, and closeness that Jesus is offering you. Let Jesus comfort you. He can and will comfort you through your hurt, pain, and brokenness. Open your heart and receive His comfort. Jesus is wrapping His arms around you in this moment. My challenge to you is embrace Jesus's comfort.

Stamina to REAP

Respond to Scripture: This is the familiarize yourself with the scripture stage.

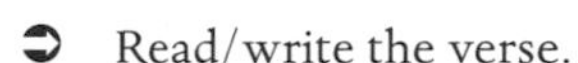

- ➲ Read/write the verse.

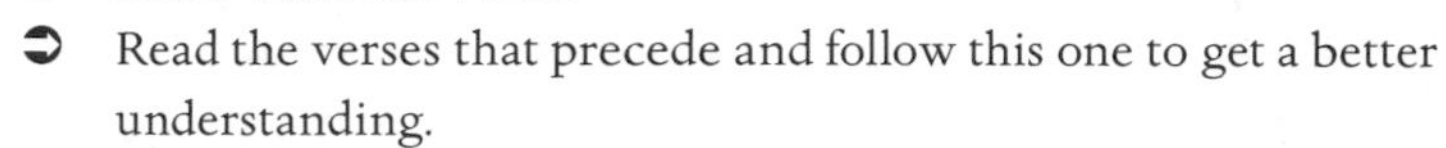

- ➲ Read the verses that precede and follow this one to get a better understanding.

> Though you have made me see troubles, many and bitter, you will restore my life again; from the depths of the earth you will again bring me up. You will increase my honor and comfort me once more. (Psalm 71:20–21 NIV)

Engage: This is the meditation stage.

- ➲ What words stand out to you the most?
- ➲ What commands do you see?
- ➲ What principles do you see?

Apply: This is preparation for real-life application.

- How can you apply the scripture to your life?
- How can you apply this scripture/devotion to your daily walk with God?

Pray: Talk to God about what you learned.

- Have a conversation with God about what you learned. Ask Him to guide you by showing you how to apply this verse to your life.
- Ask God to show you His truths and promises.
- Write out what God is speaking to you. Live it out by *standing* on His *promises.*

Journal other thoughts/insights

Section 1 Prayer

Heavenly Father,

Thank you for your wisdom. I know that you know about all my struggles, cares, worries, and concerns. I have lamented, cried out, and laid all my concerns at your feet. Thank you for never leaving me during tough times or good times. Though I have had many setbacks, You have been there through it all, and I thank you. Continue to provide me with Your divine strength, endurance, and courage as I continue this journey. In Jesus's name, Amen.

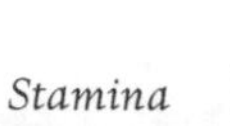

Section 2

EMBRACING GOD'S PROMISES THROUGH HIS CHARACTER

INTRODUCTION

But you, Lord, are a compassionate and gracious God,
slow to anger, abounding in love and faithfulness.
—PSALM 86:15 NIV

Hey sister,

Part one of the journey has ended. You lamented, cried out, and laid down your burdens. It is now time to move on to the next destination of your journey. You are going to walk through some of the promises of God. You may have read about God's promises. In this next section, we will look at His promises through His character. Think about it.

God's promises are love, grace, compassion, mercy, forgiveness, and faithfulness.

God is loving, graceful, compassionate, merciful, forgiving, and faithful.

In this section, you will study and understand a few of God's promises through His character.

Day 6

EVERLASTING LOVE

May your unfailing love come to me, Lord, your salvation, according to your promise.
—PSALM 119:41 NIV

Love. Love is that thing that we crave. We long to be loved and to feel loved. As humans, we are wired to feel. Most of us live through our emotions and feelings. When we feel loved, we feel safe, secure, wanted, and validated. When we do not feel loved, we feel lonely, depressed, and rejected.

To truly understand love is to understand how love is defined. *Love* is an action, not a feeling. *Love* is described as an affection based on admiration.[5] Therefore, feeling loved is different from knowing that you are loved.

God is the author of love. God loves you. There is no love greater than His love. I understand that it can sometimes be hard to believe that God loves you because we long for a physical sign of being loved. It is easier to feel or believe that you are loved when there is someone showering you with affection or telling you that you are loved. My sweet sister, take heart. God loves you more than you can ever imagine. God promised His love to you by sending His *only* son to die for your sins.

---

[5] Dictionary.com, s.v. "Love," accessed June 30, 2022, http://dictionary.reference.com/browse/love.

> For this is how God loved the world: He gave his one and only Son, so that everyone who believes in him will not perish but have eternal life. (John 3:16 NLT)

Can you imagine willingly giving up your only child to save anyone, especially a world full of sinners? As a mother of *one* child, I am pretty sure that I am not willing to give up my *only* child to save a sinful world.

God loves you with an everlasting love. *Everlasting* means continuing for a long time or indefinitely.[6] God is faithful to you as He shows you an everlasting love (Jeremiah 31:3 ESV). No love compares to God's everlasting love. God lavishes His love on you (1 John 3:1 NIV). To *lavish* means "to give something profusely or in excess".[7]

Wow! I get excited to know that God gives His love in excess. God gives you overflowing and abounding love. Therefore, it is more important to *know that you are loved* than to *feel you are loved*. Take heart, my sister. Nothing, I mean absolutely nothing, can separate you from God's love. No demon in hell, no negative thoughts, no abusive words, no fears, no worries, and no powers of darkness can do this (Romans 8:37–39 NIV). This is how much God loves you.

God's love will never give up on you. God's love will never fail you. When you start to feel unloved, read the Scriptures throughout this devotional to help you remember and know that you are loved. God's overwhelming and unfailing love carries and sustains you. God cherishes you through His everlasting love. This is who He is. This is what love is. God is love.

---

[6] Dictionary.com, s.v. "Everlasting," accessed June 30, 2022, http://dictionary.reference.com/browse/everlasting.

[7] Dictionary.com, s.v. "Lavish," accessed June 30, 2022, http://dictionary.reference.com/browse/lavish.

Stamina to REAP

Respond to Scripture: This is the familiarize yourself with the scripture stage.

- Read/write the verse.
- Read the verses that precede and follow this one to get a better understanding.

May your unfailing love come to me, Lord, your salvation, according to your promise; God lavishes his love on us. (Psalm 119:41 NIV)

Engage: This is the meditation stage.

- What words stand out to you the most?
- What commands do you see?
- What principles do you see?

Apply: This is preparation for real-life application.

- How can you apply the scripture to your life?
- How can you apply this scripture/devotion to your daily walk with God?

Pray: Talk to God about what you learned.

- Have a conversation with God about what you learned. Ask Him to guide you by showing you how to apply this verse to your life.
- Ask God to show you His truths and promises.
- Write out what God is speaking to you. Live it out by *standing* on His *promises.*

Journal other thoughts/insights

Day 7
INFINITE GRACE

You then, my child, be strengthened by the grace that is in Christ Jesus.
—2 TIMOTHY 2:1 ESV

I felt distressed, overwhelmed, and ashamed. I felt like a failure. How could I make the same mistake? What was wrong with me? How could I be so stupid? I wanted to pray, but I was ashamed. All I could do was ask Jesus to take away all the frustrations. The anxiety built up and I needed comfort and peace. I had no words to pray, so I opened my Bible. This is what I saw.

> Three times I pleaded with the Lord to take it away from me. But he said to me, "My grace is sufficient for you, for my power is made perfect in weakness." Therefore, I will boast all the more gladly about my weaknesses, so that Christ's power may rest on me. (2 Corinthians 12:8–9 NIV)

My mouth dropped in utter disbelief. This was not the verse that I was looking for. I was looking for peace and comfort. My soul wanted relief. But this is the verse that I *needed to read* at the time. God was showing me that He was not going to remove the circumstance or my frustrations at that time, but that through His *grace,* I would be given the strength to endure the circumstance and handle my frustrations.

Grace is an undeserved favor, gift, or blessing given to us by Jesus. Grace is Jesus giving us what we do not deserve.[8]

---

[8] Mark Altrogge, "The Glorious Difference Between Grace and Mercy," Bible Study Tools, posted July 8, 2021, https://www.biblestudytools.com/bible-study/topical-studies/the-glorious-life-altering-difference-between-grace-and-mercy.html.

When I fail, mess up, or fall short, I am hard on myself. Society tells me that I am a failure. Jesus tells me that His grace is sufficient. We are humans and we will stumble. Grace is extended to us not because of any remarkable thing we have done. Grace is not extended to us because we are such great people. It is in Jesus's nature to give us grace. We should give ourselves grace as well. There is no perfection in any of us. Since there is no perfection in any of us, we should be open to extending grace to others as well.

Sister, trade your failures, shame, and shortcomings for God's goodness and grace. This is who He is. God is graceful.

Stamina to REAP

Respond to Scripture: This is the familiarize yourself with the scripture stage.

- Read/write the verse.
- Read the verses that precede and follow this one to get a better understanding.

You then, my child, be strengthened by the grace that is in Christ Jesus. (2 Timothy 2:1 ESV)

Engage: This is the meditation stage.

- What words stand out to you the most?
- What commands do you see?
- What principles do you see?

Apply: This is preparation for real-life application.

- How can you apply the scripture to your life?
- How can you apply this scripture/devotion to your daily walk with God?

Pray: Talk to God about what you learned.

- Have a conversation with God about what you learned. Ask Him to guide you by showing you how to apply this verse to your life.
- Ask God to show you His truths and promises.
- Write out what God is speaking to you. Live it out by *standing* on His *promises.*

Journal other thoughts/insights

Day 8

ABUNDANT MERCY

For You, Lord, are good, and ready to forgive, And abundant in mercy to all those who call upon You.
—PSALM 86:5 NKJV

"Have mercy on me." You may have heard this statement. You may have made this statement yourself. What exactly are we asking for when we ask for mercy? Mercy is when God gives us what we do not deserve.[9] God demonstrates his favor, love, and compassion through mercy.

God wants us to be happy and successful. He wants us to have an abundant life (John 10:10 ESV). God does not continue to count our failures and wrongdoings. Through his mercy, each day that we wake up, we are given the opportunity to try again (Lamentations 3:22-23 ESV). We are given the opportunity to move forward.

It is through God's mercy that we can forgive ourselves and others. Sweet sister, whatever regret, guilt, or shame that you are holding on to today, let it go. Whatever bitterness or resentment you are holding toward someone else, let it go. God forgives us, but we must also forgive others (Matthew 6:15 ESV). It is not worth expending your energy or not receiving your own forgiveness. Grant others mercy. Let it go. Sister, embrace God's mercy and forgiveness. God is merciful and forgiving to us. This is who He is.

---

[9] Altrogge, "The Glorious Difference Between Grace and Mercy."

Stamina to REAP

Respond to Scripture: This is the familiarize yourself with the scripture stage.

- Read/write the verse.
- Read the verses that precede and follow this one to get a better understanding.

For You, Lord, are good, and ready to forgive, And abundant in mercy to all those who call upon You. (Psalm 86:5 NKJV)

Engage: This is the meditation stage.

- What words stand out to you the most?
- What commands do you see?
- What principles do you see?

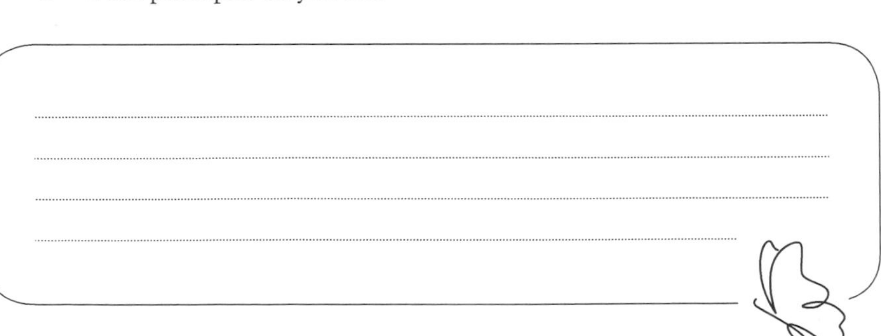

Apply: This is preparation for real-life application.

- How can you apply the scripture to your life?
- How can you apply this scripture/devotion to your daily walk with God?

Pray: Talk to God about what you learned.

- Have a conversation with God about what you learned. Ask Him to guide you by showing you how to apply this verse to your life.
- Ask God to show you His truths and promises.
- Write out what God is speaking to you. Live it out by *standing* on His *promises*.

Journal other thoughts/insights

Day 9
TRUE COMPASSION

But you, Lord, are a compassionate and gracious God,
slow to anger, abounding in love and faithfulness.
—PSALM 86:15 NIV

Compassion is one of Jesus's greatest characteristics. Jesus cares about you and your feelings. One of my favorite stories about Jesus's compassion is when he feeds over 5,000 men, women, and children.

> Jesus called his disciples to him and said, "I have compassion for these people; they have already been with me three days and have nothing to eat. I do not want to send them away hungry, or they may collapse on the way." His disciples answered, "Where could we get enough bread in this remote place to feed such a crowd?" "How many loaves do you have?" Jesus asked. "Seven," they replied, "and a few small fish." He told the crowd to sit down on the ground. Then he took the seven loaves and the fish, and when he had given thanks, he broke them and gave them to the disciples, and they in turn to the people. They all ate and were satisfied. Afterward the disciples picked up seven basketfuls of broken pieces that were left over. The number of those who ate was four thousand men, besides women and children. (Matthew 15:32–38 NIV)

Jesus performed a miracle through His compassion. In verse 32, Jesus states, "I have compassion for these people." I love how he says, "I do

not want to send them away hungry, or they may collapse." This gets me excited because I know that Jesus has compassion for me each time I feel weary, frustrated, sad, angry, or lonely. It gives me comfort to know that Jesus does not want me to be weary or "to collapse." Jesus has this same compassion for you. The very character of Jesus is compassion. He understands that you are weary. He understands the heaviness of your heart. Jesus understands your brokenness. He understands your desire and longing for more. Jesus surrounds you with compassion. My sister, allow Jesus to saturate you with His compassion. Allow His compassion to nurture you and soothe your soul. Jesus

will never let you faint. Accept His true compassion. This is who He is. Jesus is compassionate.

Stamina to REAP

Respond to Scripture: This is the familiarize yourself with the scripture stage.

- Read/write the verse.
- Read the verses that precede and follow this one to get a better understanding.

But you, Lord, are a compassionate and gracious God, Slow to anger, abounding in love and faithfulness. (Psalm 86:15 NIV)

Engage: This is the meditation stage.

- What words stand out to you the most?
- What commands do you see?
- What principles do you see?

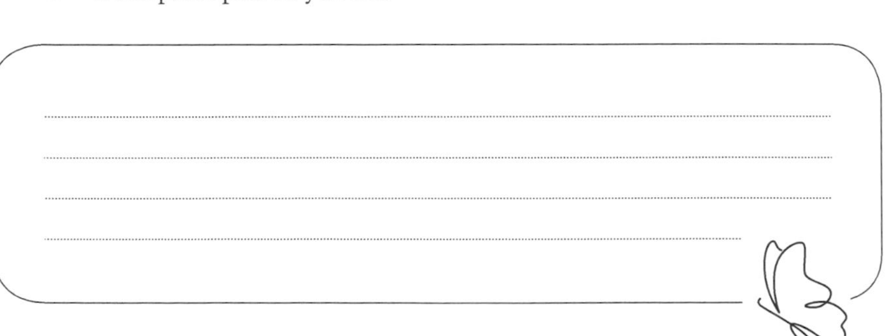

Apply: This is preparation for real-life application.

- How can you apply the scripture to your life?
- How can you apply this scripture/devotion to your daily walk with God?

Pray: Talk to God about what you learned.

- Have a conversation with God about what you learned. Ask Him to guide you by showing you how to apply this verse to your life.
- Ask God to show you His truths and promises.
- Write out what God is speaking to you. Live it out by *standing* on His *promises.*

Journal other thoughts/insights

Day 10

TOTALLY FAITHFUL

For the word of the Lord is right and true; he is faithful in all he does.
—PSALM 33:4 NIV

I stood in the doorway, watching the white moving truck roll away. He was gone. Just like that, the marriage was over. I was heartbroken, frustrated, and downright hurt. I was left with many unhappy memories, shame, and a five-year-old daughter to care for on my own. With my immediate family living over 650 miles away, all I could wonder was, *What do I do now?* Unable to control the waterfall of tears rushing from my face, I threw myself onto the couch. I continued to sob uncontrollably. *Why is this happening to me? After all, I did everything I could to make the marriage work.*

Sobbing had become part of my daily routine for several months. I would wake up and go to bed crying. I would cry while going to and coming from work. During one of my quiet times, I heard a small voice say, "Trust me. I will never leave you." I did not understand it at the time.

I was consumed with doubt, fear, shame, and worry. Concern about being able to pay the bills plagued my mind. Thoughts about what others would think about me being a divorced, single mother took over my mind. I worried about the impact the divorce would have on my daughter. I felt like a failure. I was tired and exhausted. At that point, I was just surviving from day to day. I know that God said he would never leave me alone, but it was very hard to believe on most days.

A little while later, I was laid off from my job. The stress of it all had become too much for me to bear. There were days when I did not have enough money for food. Bills did not stop coming. Pink disconnection notices arrived every month for at least six months. I drained my savings account. But God was so faithful to my daughter and me. Nothing in our home was ever disconnected, not even luxuries such as cable and internet. God was truly there for us through it all. God did not make it all go away immediately, but He did not leave me. He was there the whole time. God continued to show His faithfulness to me. Bills were paid and caught up eventually. This was a turning point for my faith. This is where I had to truly search my heart to reveal how much I really trusted God and his faithfulness. It was then that I understood what God meant when He whispered to me that He would never leave. Now when things are tough or I start to lose faith, I meditate on this verse.

> The Lord himself goes before you and will be with you
> he will never leave you nor forsake you. Do not be afraid;
> do not be discouraged. (Deuteronomy 31:8 NIV)

God may not release you from the circumstance immediately, but He will continue to demonstrate His faithfulness in your life. God is faithful. This is who He is.

Stamina to REAP

Respond to Scripture: This is the familiarize yourself with the scripture stage.

- Read/write the verse.
- Read the verses that precede and follow this one to get a better understanding.

For the word of the Lord is right and true; he is faithful in all he does. (Psalm 33:4 NIV)

Engage: This is the meditation stage.

- What words stand out to you the most?
- What commands do you see?
- What principles do you see?

Apply: This is preparation for real-life application.

- How can you apply the scripture to your life?
- How can you apply this scripture/devotion to your daily walk with God?

Pray: Talk to God about what you learned.

- Have a conversation with God about what you learned. Ask Him to guide you by showing you how to apply this verse to your life.
- Ask God to show you His truths and promises.
- Write out what God is speaking to you. Live it out by *standing* on His *promises.*

Journal other thoughts/insights

Section 2 Prayer

Heavenly Father,

Thank you for your love, grace, mercy, forgiveness, and compassion. You are an awesome and mighty God. I do not want to take your love, compassion, grace, and mercy for granted. Please forgive me for all my sins, both intentional and unintentional. Help me to be quick to forgive others, as you forgive me. Thank you for loving me. In Jesus's name, Amen.

Section 3
REVIVE YOUR SOUL

INTRODUCTION

My soul clings to the dust; Revive me according to Your word.
—PSALM 119:25 NKJV

My sister,

It is time to do some heart work. You are now at the point in your journey where you will open your heart and get vulnerable. Allow God to comfort, strengthen, and guide you on your journey of renewal and restoration. It is time for your weary heart and soul to heal. Your crushed spirit and brokenness will be transformed into wholeness. You will be tasked with allowing God's guidance to come in to heal and restore those areas where you are experiencing weariness, weakness, or brokenness.

This process will not be easy, but it is necessary to move forward in the journey. We will do it together. I am excited to be on this journey with you! Let's go!

Day 11
YOU MATTER

For you formed my inward parts; you knitted me together in my mother's womb. I praise you, for I am fearfully and wonderfully made. Wonderful are your works; my soul knows it very well.
—PSALM 139:13–14 ESV

> Feeling invisible. Feeling like no one cares. I pray. I try to have the faith to believe that someone would come along who cares. God are you there? Can you save me? I don't fit in. I have never fit in. I'm not a good mom. I have no friends. I am always failing. Save me. Teach me how to be a better me. I'm in bondage and I want to be freed. Help me God. My heart is broken. I feel so alone. I feel like I don't fit in anywhere. Where can I run and hide? Please help me. I'm crying out to you. Please hear me.

This is a written prayer that I wrote out/cried out to the Lord some years ago. This was my lament. This was me feeling worthless, as a mother and as a person. Due to a history of trauma, it was hard for me to accept that I was good enough. It was hard for me to accept that I was important to God. I could not understand why the *mighty* and *awesome* God would care about me. I continued to read scriptures about how God feels about me. I was able to go through each day a little differently. Even now on my most difficult days, I must still remember that I am fearfully and wonderfully made (Psalm 139:14 ESV)

Failure, disappointment, hurt, anxiety, and shame can often leave us feeling as if we are not enough. Through the disappointment and weariness of our souls, we can lose our sense of identity.

You are important to God. You matter. Your life on this earth has purpose and meaning. God has a plan for your life (Jeremiah 29:11 NIV), no matter how many detours or backroads you have taken. He cares about all your thoughts, feelings, emotions, and your well-being.

Remember who you are to God.

On your hardest days, recite this poem and let it soak in that you matter to God.

> I am loved (1 John 3:1 NIV)
> I am unique (Ephesians 2:10 NIV)
> I am strong (Ephesians 6:10 ESV)
> I am the apple of His eye (Psalm 17:8 ESV)
> I am brave (Philippians 4:13 NKJV)
> I am valuable (Matthew 6:26 NIV)
> I am fearfully and wonderfully made (Psalm 139:14 ESV)
> I have a purpose (Psalm 138:8 ESV)
> I am enough (Zephaniah 3:17 NLT)

My dear sister, you matter to God.

Stamina to REAP

Respond to Scripture: This is the familiarize yourself with the scripture stage.

- Read/write the verse.
- Read the verses that precede and follow this one to get a better understanding.

For you formed my inward parts, you knitted me together in my mother's womb. I praise you, for I am fearfully and wonderfully made. Wonderful are your works my soul knows it very well. (Psalm 139:13–14 ESV)

Engage: This is the meditation stage.

- What words stand out to you the most?
- What commands do you see?
- What principles do you see?

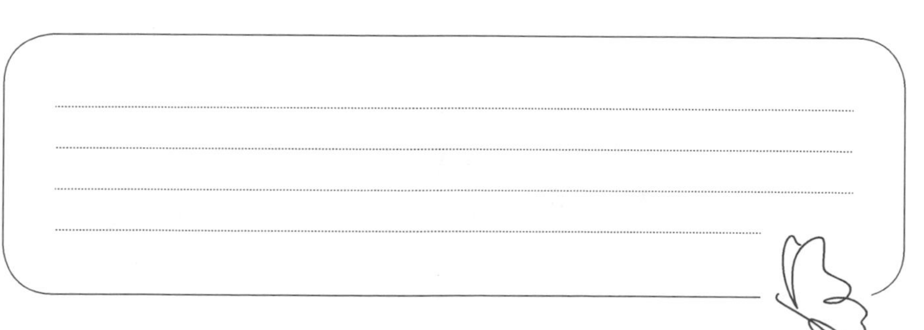

Apply: This is preparation for real-life application.

- How can you apply the scripture to your life?
- How can you apply this scripture/devotion to your daily walk with God?

Pray: Talk to God about what you learned.

- Have a conversation with God about what you learned. Ask Him to guide you by showing you how to apply this verse to your life.
- Ask God to show you His truths and promises.
- Write out what God is speaking to you. Live it out by *standing* on His *promises.*

Journal other thoughts/insights

Day 12

AWAKEN YOUR SPIRIT

For he satisfies the longing soul, and the hungry soul he fills with good things.
—PSALM 107:9 ESV

I awoke suddenly from a short rest, as I had tossed and turned most of the night. I was excited. It was vacation time. For the past four years, I talked about going to South Carolina. Looking at pictures, I thought South Carolina was such a beautiful place. There was this passion and burning desire deep down inside to visit, maybe even move there. The time had now come. We arrived at the airport for our 8:00 a.m. flight. As I boarded the plane, my soul was aroused. My heart was doing cartwheels. I could feel the spark in my spirit.

Hurt, shame, feelings of failure, and weariness lead to bitterness and closing off our hearts to others. Sometimes we find ourselves closing our hearts to God as well. Stirring up of the spirit and soul is needed. Our spirit is crying out for something deeper. An undeniable passion burns within us and longs to be quenched. Our souls need refreshing. Our spirits need reviving. We need to feel alive again. God is a restorer. He is a healer. God will restore you to a better version of yourself if you allow Him to. The brokenness, hurt, and guilt are not who you are; they are just parts of the journey. God will breathe life into your spirit and make you feel alive again.

> And I will give you a new heart, and a new spirit I will put within you. And I will remove the heart of stone from

your flesh And give you a heart of flesh.
(Ezekiel 36:26 ESV)

The burdensome feelings and heaviness of the soul are extraordinary and can lead to feelings of frustration, discouragement, desperation, and hopelessness. Therefore, go to God and ask Him to stir up your spirit. Ask God to help you snap out of the feelings of being stuck. He is the only one who can re-energize that spark and make you feel alive again. It is this spark, arousal, and excitement you feel when your spirit is awakened.

Stamina to REAP

Respond to Scripture: This is the familiarize yourself with the scripture stage.

- Read/write the verse.
- Read the verses that precede and follow this one to get a better understanding.

For he satisfies the longing soul, and the hungry soul he fills with good things. (Psalm 107:9 ESV)

Engage: This is the meditation stage.

- What words stand out to you the most?
- What commands do you see?
- What principles do you see?

Apply: This is preparation for real-life application.

- ➲ How can you apply the scripture to your life?
- ➲ How can you apply this scripture/devotion to your daily walk with God?

Pray: Talk to God about what you learned.

- ➲ Have a conversation with God about what you learned. Ask Him to guide you by showing you how to apply this verse to your life.
- ➲ Ask God to show you His truths and promises.
- ➲ Write out what God is speaking to you. Live it out by *standing* on His *promises.*

Journal other thoughts/insights

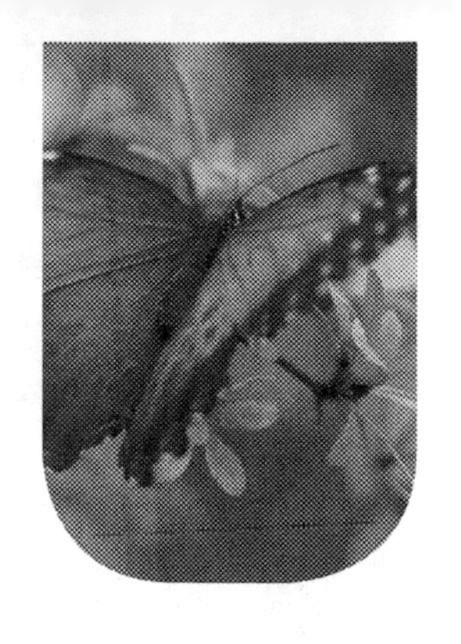

Day 13
DETOXIFY YOUR MIND

Don't copy the behavior and customs of this world, but let God transform you into a new person by changing the way you think. Then you will learn to know God's will for you, which is good and pleasing and perfect.
—ROMANS 12:2 NLT

Why do I have to suffer while others are living their best lives? I have a life full of heartbreak, loneliness, and chaos. This is what I used to think. It is not a good feeling. It is often said that if you want a good life, you must make it. Seriously, is it that easy? Sometimes it can be hard to get past the chaos, unfairness, and inequality. The noise inside your head can get quite loud. These negative thoughts, criticism, and self-doubt are hard to get rid of.

Negative thoughts, anxiety, and doubt can plague your mind, especially when dealing with hardships. Bad experiences, rejection, and failures contribute to negative thinking. Some of those bad experiences play over and over in your mind. Those replays make you feel unworthy of Jesus's love and your relationship with Him. Trust in Jesus allows you to be free from the guilt of the past and negative thinking. Jesus does not want you to be caught up in thoughts of your past and your failures.

It is human nature to have negative thoughts, especially when things are not going your way. The key is to focus on Jesus and ask Him to help give you a mind filled with peace and positive thoughts. Do not stay

stuck in stinking thinking. Renew your mind. This means being intentional about positive thinking. This means letting go of negative and toxic thinking. You are a conqueror of your negative thoughts. You will overcome the negative mindset. Even when those thoughts come in again, you will put them to rest because you know who you are in Christ.

Stamina to REAP

Respond to Scripture: This is the familiarize yourself with the scripture stage.

- Read/write the verse.

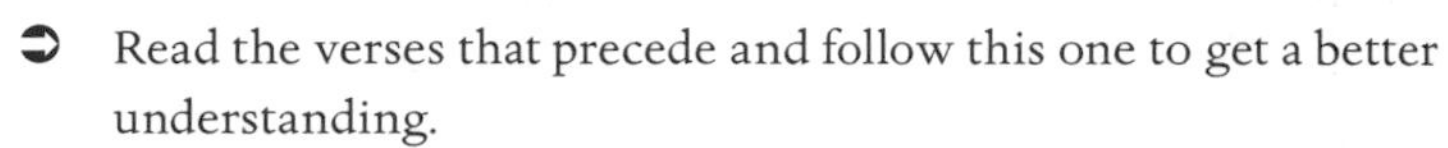

- Read the verses that precede and follow this one to get a better understanding.

> Don't copy the behavior and customs of this world, but let God transform you into a new person by changing the way you think. Then you will learn to know God's will for you, which is good and pleasing and perfect. (Romans 12:2 NLT)

Engage: This is the meditation stage.

- What words stand out to you the most?
- What commands do you see?
- What principles do you see?

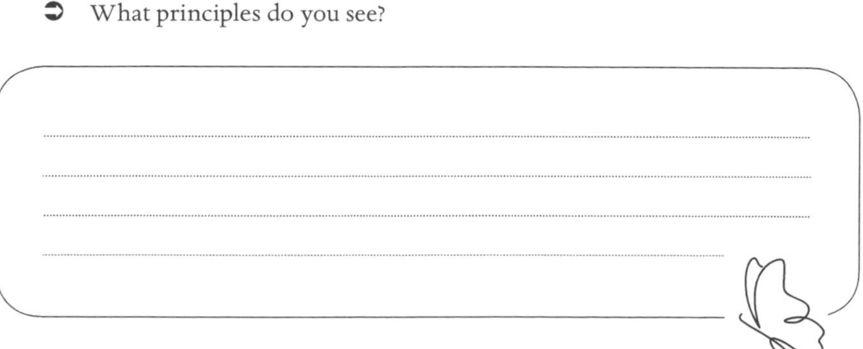

Apply: This is preparation for real-life application.

- How can you apply the scripture to your life?
- How can you apply this scripture/devotion to your daily walk with God?

Pray: Talk to God about what you learned.

- Have a conversation with God about what you learned. Ask Him to guide you by showing you how to apply this verse to your life.
- Ask God to show you His truths and promises.
- Write out what God is speaking to you. Live it out by *standing* on His *promises*.

Journal other thoughts/insights

Day 14

RISE ABOVE REJECTION

What shall we say to these things? If God is for us, who can be against us?
—ROMANS 8:31 ESV

My father was not a part of my life as I was growing up. At the age of thirty, I reconnected with him. My father and I talked on the phone for about two months, as he lives out of state. We had two brief in-person interactions. One day, I asked my father if we could have a conversation about why he chose not to be involved in my life. He said sure and he wanted to talk in person. I never heard from him again. There I was, rejected by my *own father*—again. Several years later, and still not a word from my father. The sting of the rejection hurts as much now as it did when I was a child and ten years ago.

> Even if my father and mother abandon me, the LORD will hold me close. (Psalm 27:10 NLT)

Some of our deepest hurts are formed through some type of rejection. Although rejection is a natural part of life, the pain and hurt it causes is not easy to handle. Rejection can come from those closest to us, or those we are trying to build a relationship with. I think rejection hurts so much because most times we just want to be acknowledged. We long for someone to acknowledge our thoughts and feelings. We are looking for a sense of belonging.

Rejection can make us feel unwanted and not good enough. Being rejected only once can cause fear that you will be rejected all the time. Negative thoughts can creep into your mind and make it appear as if you are being rejected by everyone. If you allow those negative thoughts to manifest, you can be taken to be a very dark place. Yes, rejection and the fear of rejection can do this. I know this from experience.

But there is good news! Jesus is a healer. He is here to help you through the fear of rejection and the rejection itself. When feeling rejected, it can be hard to believe that Jesus is with you. But trust me sister, He is with you. Jesus was rejected by his *own people.*

> He came into the very world he created, but the world didn't recognize him. He came to his own people, and even they rejected him. (John 1:10–11 NLT)

Although rejected, Jesus did not let the rejection distract or deter him from His purpose. His purpose was to die on the cross so that you and I can be saved. Do not allow the fear of rejection stop you from moving forward. The enemy wants you to be fearful and not move forward in your purpose.

The next time you are rejected by someone, or feel that you will be rejected, take a deep breath. Ask Jesus for His peace to guard your heart and your mind. You will not allow rejection or the fear of rejection to distract you from moving forward in your purpose. Move forward. Rise above the rejection! Jesus is always on your side!

Stamina to REAP

Respond to Scripture: This is the familiarize yourself with the scripture stage.

- Read/write the verse.
- Read the verses that precede and follow this one to get a better understanding.

> What shall we say to these things? If God is for us, who can be against us? (Romans 8:31 ESV)

Engage: This is the meditation stage.

- What words stand out to you the most?
- What commands do you see?
- What principles do you see?

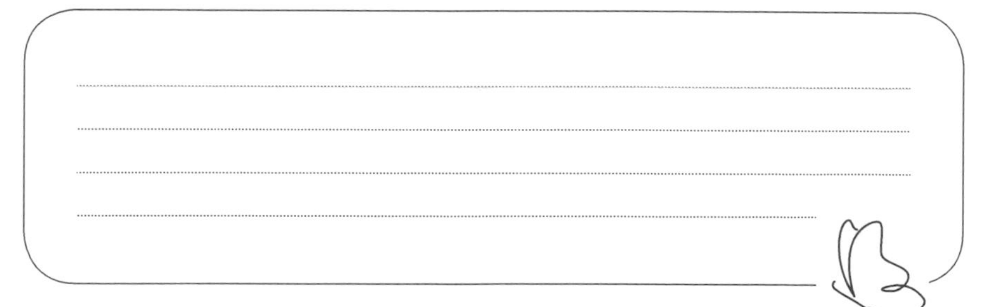

Apply: This is preparation for real-life application.

- How can you apply the scripture to your life?
- How can you apply this scripture/devotion to your daily walk with God?

Pray: Talk to God about what you learned.

- Have a conversation with God about what you learned. Ask Him to guide you by showing you how to apply this verse to your life.
- Ask God to show you His truths and promises.
- Write out what God is speaking to you. Live it out by *standing* on His *promises.*

Journal other thoughts/insights

Day 15

JUST BREATHE

Do not be anxious about anything, but in every situation, by prayer and petition, with thanksgiving, present your requests to God. And the peace of God, which transcends all understanding, will guard your hearts and your minds in Christ Jesus.
—PHILIPPIANS 4:6–7 NIV

A weight is upon my shoulders. It is hard to breathe. This is a feeling that I have endured most of my life. Most days, I wake up and fall asleep crying. My heart beats rapidly as my mind races. There are so many what-ifs and whys. This is what it feels like for a person filled with worry and anxiety. I worried about everything from not having enough to not being good enough. Yep, that was me.

Now I choose to fight worry and anxiety. As my faith gets stronger, my worries and anxieties get weaker. It is my faith in God that allows me to be free from the struggles of worry and anxiety. I am being healed and set free from these things. My faith gives me the freedom to know that no matter what situation I face, God will always be there for me. As my faith grows, so does my confidence in God.

Stress is inevitable, but constant worry, stress, and anxiety is not healthy. God wants us to give our cares, worry, and stress to Him (1 Peter 5:7 NLT). Anxiety and stress will take a toll on your body and cause physical ailments. Do not be consumed with worry and anxiety. God is in control of your life. Continue to grow your relationship with Him. Trust him to take care of everything that you are going through and everything that

you will go through. If you suffer from constant anxiety and stress, find ways to decompress.

I have listed some of my favorite way to decompress.

- Practice deep breathing techniques.
- Take walks in nature and actually stop to smell the roses or lilies.
- Listen to music.
- Listen to the Bible.
- Listen to an audiobook.
- Sit by the water.
- Treat yourself every once and a while.
- Have a cup of coffee or lunch with a friend.
- Believe in yourself. You got this.

Stamina to REAP

Respond to Scripture: This is the familiarize yourself with the scripture stage.

- Read/write the verse.
- Read the verses that precede and follow this one to get a better understanding.

> Do not be anxious about anything, but in every situation, by prayer and petition, with thanksgiving, present your requests to God. And the peace of God, which transcends all understanding, will guard your hearts and your minds in Christ Jesus. (Philippians 4:6–7 NIV)

Engage: This is the meditation stage.

- What words stand out to you the most?
- What commands do you see?
- What principles do you see?

Apply: This is preparation for real-life application.

- How can you apply the scripture to your life?
- How can you apply this scripture/devotion to your daily walk with God?

Pray: Talk to God about what you learned.

- Have a conversation with God about what you learned. Ask Him to guide you by showing you how to apply this verse to your life.
- Ask God to show you His truths and promises.
- Write out what God is speaking to you. Live it out by *standing* on His *promises.*

Journal other thoughts/insights

Section 3 Prayer

Heavenly Father,

Thank You for the revival of my soul. Thank You for allowing your Holy Spirit to awaken my spirit and detoxify my mind. I am learning who I am in you. I want to hold fast the understanding of who I am in you. I know that You love me and care for me. Please help me to maintain positive thoughts. Help me to continue to seek You when I am feeling rejected or anxious. Thank You for Your compassion and kindness that You bestow upon me when I call You.

In Jesus's name, Amen.

Section 4

YOU GOT THIS

INTRODUCTION

And after you have suffered a little while, the God of all grace, who has called you to his eternal glory in Christ, will himself restore, confirm, strengthen, and establish you.
—1 PETER 5:10 ESV

My darling sister,

You did it! You made it to the final leg of this journey. You laid down your burdens and cried out to Jesus. You embraced Jesus's promises. You opened your heart and allowed Him to restore, strengthen, and establish your spirit and mind. Your hard work has paid off.

In this final section, you will embrace the strength and stamina needed to move forward and conquer life, no matter the hardships. Trials and struggles come to build character and make you stronger. When finished with this section, you will move forward with your mind, heart, and soul renewed. You will keep the faith and not lose heart. God's wisdom and understanding will guide you through hardships and setbacks.

Day 16

RENEWED HOPE

Hope deferred makes the heart sick, but a desire fulfilled is a tree of life.
—PROVERBS 13:12 ESV

Hope is the longing to have a need or desire fulfilled. Have you ever put your hope in someone or something, only to be disappointed that the situation did not turn out the way you expected it to? Wait, let me rephrase that question. How *many times* have you put your hope in someone or something only to be disappointed when the situation did not turn out the way you expected it to? Hope is anticipating, trusting, or believing that something will happen. Hope is powerful.

Life is both challenging and amazing. It is through hope and faith that we fight through the challenging to get to the amazing. Through hope, we look forward to breakthroughs, miracles, or blessings that are not yet seen. It is hope that motivates and drives us to keep moving forward. You will never be put to shame when your hope lies in God (Psalm 25:3 NIV). Never lose hope in God, no matter how tough a situation or circumstance may seem. God will give you peace and joy when you place your hope in Him (Romans 15:13 NIV).

In your darkest moments, *choose hope*!
During a financial crisis, *choose hope*!
When coping with relationship problems, *choose hope*!

God will give you strength, courage, and comfort as you hope in Him. Hope is strengthened when you continue to focus on the promises of God (Romans 15:4 ESV). My darling sister, keep going. Let your heart cling to hope.

Stamina to REAP

Respond to Scripture: This is the familiarize yourself with the scripture stage.

- Read/write the verse.
- Read the verses that precede and follow this one to get a better understanding.

Hope deferred makes the heart sick, but a desire fulfilled is a tree of life. (Proverbs 13:12 ESV)

Engage: This is the meditation stage.

- What words stand out to you the most?
- What commands do you see?
- What principles do you see?

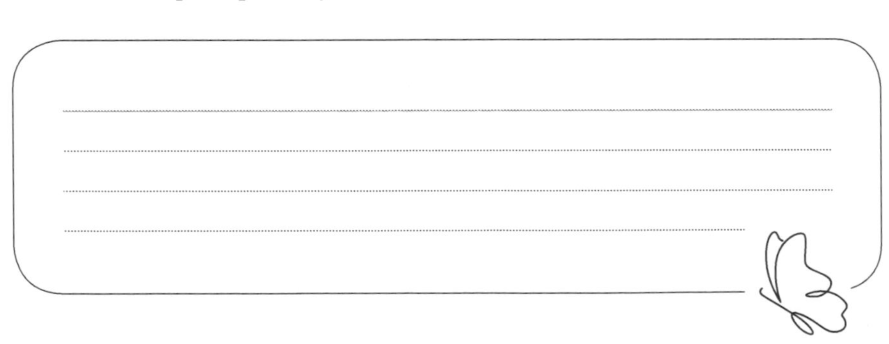

Apply: This is preparation for real-life application.

- How can you apply the scripture to your life?
- How can you apply this scripture/devotion to your daily walk with God?

Pray: Talk to God about what you learned.

- Have a conversation with God about what you learned. Ask Him to guide you by showing you how to apply this verse to your life.
- Ask God to show you His truths and promises.
- Write out what God is speaking to you. Live it out by *standing* on His *promises.*

Journal other thoughts/insights

Day 17

SUSTAINING FAITH

Now faith is confidence in what we hope for and assurance about what we do not see.
—HEBREWS 11:1 NIV

One typical Thursday morning, I awoke to throbbing leg pain. I took Advil and headed to work. After a few hours at work, I felt a severe pain in the back of my right leg. I took Tylenol and went on with my day. On Saturday morning, the pain continued, and I thought I just needed to walk it off. I completed my routine Saturday morning walk and errands. By Sunday morning, the pain was so intense that I could not walk. My right foot was so swollen, I could not place it on the ground. I then headed to urgent care. After an urgent care visit and two doctors' visits within five days, I was sent to the emergency room. Tests revealed blood clots in my leg. I kept saying to myself, *I do not have time to be sick. There is no room for this in my life right now.* As the weeks went by, there were more doctors' appointments and more medical bills. Other medical issues began to arise, which led to other medical procedures. Doctors were still trying to find the cause of the blood clots.

Most days, all I could do was cry because of the pain. I also cried because there was no known cause. I became discouraged. I started losing hope. I felt like as if my life was becoming unglued for six months.

My dear sister, hard times and struggles are a natural part of life. God uses hard times and struggles to build character and endurance. Hard times and struggles make us or break us. During some struggles, we may feel that we are coming unglued. This is where faith steps in. Faith is trusting and believing in something that has not been received yet. I have learned that sustaining faith is our best defense against hard times.

Ways to sustain faith:

- Pray continually.

> Pray continually, give thanks in all circumstances, for this is God's will for you in Christ Jesus. (1 Thessalonians 5:17–18 NIV)

Praying continually allows you to seek God and make your requests known to Him. Continual prayer also allows you to hear from God. Prayer is your communication with God. Praying continually helps you to listen for God's wisdom and guidance while you are going through the process. Being grateful and praising God in all circumstances shows that you have faith that God will work out the situation on your behalf.

- Stay focused on God by reading His word daily.

> Keep this Book of the Law always on your lips; meditate on it day and night, so that you may be careful to do everything written in it. Then you will be prosperous and successful. (Joshua 1:8 NIV)

God's Word provides His promises. Faith is built and sustained through reading and meditating on His Word. It is through His Word that we learn how to trust the process.

- Remember your previous victories.

> I will remember the deeds of the LORD; yes, I will remember your miracles of long ago. (Psalm 77:11 NIV)

God will always see you through the hard times. Think back to a time when you were going through a hard time and God came through. This is the reassurance that you need that He will do it time and time again. It is all about building perseverance.

God is good and His faithfulness endures forever (Psalm 100:5 NIV). No matter what trial or difficult circumstance you face, God is always there. Difficult circumstances are not fun or pleasurable, but those circumstances build our characters if we continue to trust in God and His faithfulness.

Sister, you may not see it while you are going through the struggle, but just remember that you will get through it. Cling to God. Continue to pray for His strength to get through the hardest moments. Maintain your faith and do not lose hope. God will see you through. He always does! God comes through at the right time.

Stamina to REAP

Respond to Scripture: This is the familiarize yourself with the scripture stage.

- Read/write the verse.
- Read the verses that precede and follow this one to get a better understanding.

Now faith is confidence in what we hope for and assurance about what we do not see. (Hebrews 11:1 NIV)

Engage: This is the meditation stage.

- What words stand out to you the most?
- What commands do you see?
- What principles do you see?

Apply: This is preparation for real-life application.

- How can you apply the scripture to your life?
- How can you apply this scripture/devotion to your daily walk with God?

Pray: Talk to God about what you learned.

- Have a conversation with God about what you learned. Ask Him to guide you by showing you how to apply this verse to your life.
- Ask God to show you His truths and promises.
- Write out what God is speaking to you. Live it out by *standing* on His *promises.*

Journal other thoughts/insights

Day 18

JOY IN YOUR HEART

May the God of hope fill you with all joy and peace as you trust in him,so that you may overflow with hope by the power of the Holy Spirit.
—ROMANS 15:13 NIV

I love to encourage others through my Motivational Monday posts on social media. Comments I usually get are "You are so upbeat" or "You are so happy." That is not always the case. Some Mondays, I am struggling with defeat and discouragement as well. I usually must tap into my joy. Joy is that internal euphoric feeling deep inside of me. It is a feeling that I get from the Holy Spirit. Joy is not temporal or based on circumstances. My hope and courage are strengthened through the joy in my heart.

Joy is not affected by difficult circumstances or situations. Tap into your joy to defeat discouragement and despair. Let your hope overflow from joy. Let the joy in your heart take you to another level in your praise and worship, no matter what you are dealing with. Joy and hope are weapons that will get you through your toughest days. My challenge to you is to tap into your joy during a challenge or difficult circumstance. I challenge you to tap into your joy and praise and worship God during these times. Your joy will carry you through those time times. Seek joy! It is in within you.

Stamina to REAP

Respond to Scripture: This is the familiarize yourself with the scripture stage.

- Read/write the verse.
- Read the verses that precede and follow this one to get a better understanding.

May the God of hope fill you with all joy and peace as you trust in him, so that you may overflow with hope by the power of the Holy Spirit. (Romans 15:13 NIV)

Engage: This is the meditation stage.

- What words stand out to you the most?
- What commands do you see?
- What principles do you see?

Apply: This is preparation for real-life application.

- How can you apply the scripture to your life?
- How can you apply this scripture/devotion to your daily walk with God?

Pray: Talk to God about what you learned.

- Have a conversation with God about what you learned. Ask Him to guide you by showing you how to apply this verse to your life.
- Ask God to show you His truths and promises.
- Write out what God is speaking to you. Live it out by *standing* on His *promises.*

Journal other thoughts/insights

Day 19

COURAGE TO MOVE FORWARD WITH PURPOSE

Trust in the Lord with all your heart, and do not lean on your own understanding. In all your ways acknowledge him, and he will make straight your paths.
—PROVERBS 3:5–6 ESV

I am amazed at how God plants big dreams and ideas in our hearts. These are the dreams that we definitely cannot complete or fulfill in our own strength or with our own resources. They are the dreams that we know we need God and *all* His strength and guidance to carry out. One of those dreams for me is writing. This book is seven years in the making. If I would have just trusted God and moved forward seven years ago, I may be writing book three or four right now. We have huge goals and dreams, but we get stuck in our comfort zones. We are sometimes afraid to move out of our comfort zones. When I get great ideas planted in my soul, it is usually the big F word that holds me back. Yep, you guessed it: fear. I started and stopped writing this book at least three times because of fear: fear of not being good enough, fear of the unknown, and fear of not having the resources.

God has a purpose and plan for your life. He wants you to prosper. God wants to give you hope and a future (Jeremiah 29:11 NIV). God will continue to stir up the purpose that He has planted and deposited in you. He will give you the resources and tools to accomplish the tasks and goals that He sets before you.

Sister, use your faith and courage to go after your dreams. Now is the time to move forward in your purpose. God will give you strength to get started and keep moving forward. Seek Him and listen to His voice. Your purpose involves your impact on the kingdom of God, your family, and your community. There is someone else waiting and depending on you to move forward in your purpose. Because I let go of fear and picked up courage, you are now reading my first book. God is with you. Lean on the strength of His might to carry you through. Be bold, be courageous, and be fearless. Stay committed and focused on God's purpose for your life. You have learned how to navigate the challenges and struggles of life—now go forth with courage knowing that God is with you.

Stamina to REAP

Respond to Scripture: This is the familiarize yourself with the scripture stage.

- Read/write the verse.
- Read the verses that precede and follow this one to get a better understanding.

> Trust in the Lord with all your heart, and do not lean on your own understanding. In all your ways acknowledge him, and he will make straight your paths. (Proverbs 3:5–6 ESV)

Engage: This is the meditation stage.

- What words stand out to you the most?
- What commands do you see?
- What principles do you see?

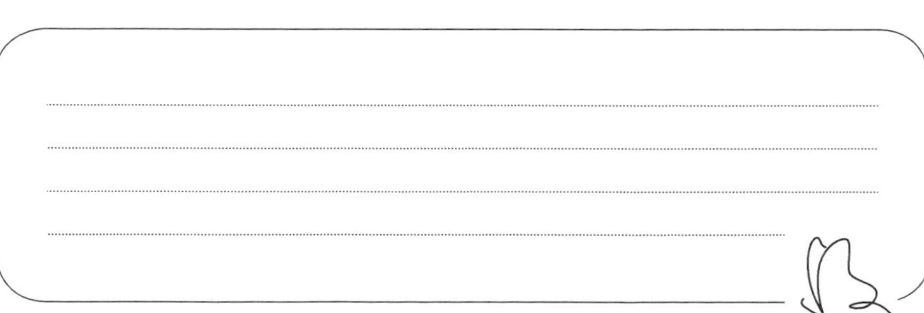

Apply: This is preparation for real-life application.

- How can you apply the scripture to your life?
- How can you apply this scripture/devotion to your daily walk with God?

Pray: Talk to God about what you learned.

- Have a conversation with God about what you learned. Ask Him to guide you by showing you how to apply this verse to your life.
- Ask God to show you His truths and promises.
- Write out what God is speaking to you. Live it out by *standing* on His *promises*.

Journal other thoughts/insights

Day 20

YOU GOT THIS

I can do all things through Christ who strengthens me.
—PHILIPPIANS 4:13 NKJV

You did it! You go girl! You have learned to lament, embrace His promises, and awaken your spirit. As I write these final words, I can just hear, "You got this. I am with you." The words "you got this" are replaying over and over in my head. God will *never* let you down. Everything may not happen *when* we want it to or *how* we want it to happen, but God will come through for us. Do not pick that weariness back up. Jesus is carrying that load that you laid at His feet. Continue to do your part by reading and meditating on His word, crying out to Him, and trusting Him.

Do not give up! Keep pushing through to your purpose. Remember, the struggles and hardships will come. When they come, remind yourself who you are in Christ. Even better, remind yourself who God is. Remind yourself of His promises and character. Remind yourself that all things are possible with God (Luke 1:37 ESV). It will take faith, tenacity, grit, strength, and endurance to make it through this life. Guess what? You have it all. It is all in you.

> Remember not the former things, nor consider the things of old. Behold, I am doing a new thing; now it springs forth, do you not perceive it? I will make a way in the wilderness and rivers in the desert. (Isaiah 43:18–19 ESV)

Your view and perception of life can help you endure the toughest times. Knowing that God can and will do great things in your life helps you

endure the trials and struggles. Do not dwell on your past. Do not look back. Keep your eyes focused on the prize that is ahead of you. God can and will do something new in your life if you let Him. He is the God of restoration, healing, and renewal. He is a miracle working God. He wants to see you happy and successful.

Say this out loud:

God is doing a new thing in my life. I am open to receiving it. I will not continue to live in the past. I will focus on looking forward to new blessings and miracles that God is going to spring forth in my life. The weariness and burdens are all laid down at Jesus's feet. I will move forward.

Stamina. You got it. I feel like chanting a cheer song for you. Embrace the stamina, strength, and renewal that you have received from God through His wisdom and this devotional.

Stamina to REAP

Respond to Scripture: This is the familiarize yourself with the scripture stage.

- Read/write the verse.
- Read the verses that precede and follow this one to get a better understanding.

I can do all things through Christ who strengthens me. (Philippians 4:13 NKJV)

Engage: This is the meditation stage.

- What words stand out to you the most?
- What commands do you see?
- What principles do you see?

Apply: This is preparation for real-life application.

- How can you apply the scripture to your life?
- How can you apply this scripture/devotion to your daily walk with God?

Pray: Talk to God about what you learned.

- Have a conversation with God about what you learned. Ask Him to guide you by showing you how to apply this verse to your life.
- Ask God to show you His truths and promises.
- Write out what God is speaking to you. Live it out by *standing* on His *promises*.

Journal other thoughts/insights

Section 4 Prayer:

Heavenly Father,

Thank you for everything that you have done in my life. Thank you for your guidance, wisdom, and peace. Please allow the words that I read to penetrate my heart and mind. Thank you for releasing me from my weariness. I lay all my hopes and dreams in your hands. In Jesus's name, Amen.

Conclusion
SHE ENDURED

She is clothed with strength and dignity; she can laugh at the days to come,
She speaks with wisdom, and faithful instruction is on her tongue.
—PROVERBS 31:25–26 NIV

When we are in uncomfortable situations and circumstances, we immediately look for a way out. It is hard for us to see or even think about the light when we are in darkness. Although it is hard to see or think about the light, the light is still there, and Jesus is present with us in our hurt.

> The light shines in the darkness, and the darkness has not overcome it. (John 1:5 ESV)

Dear sister, you do matter. You are important. You are worthy. So let those tears fall and flow. After all, God keeps those tears in a bottle. Now shake it off and go slay day after day. Not every day will be easy, but every day is manageable. You can do all things through Christ's strength. The key is tapping in and leaning on Him and His strength. Endure, my sister, endure. Persist, my sister, persist. Keep pushing through. You will not be weary when you run. You will not faint when you walk,

> but those who hope in the Lord will renew their strength. They will soar on wings like eagles; they will run and not grow weary, they will walk and not be faint. (Isaiah 40:31 NIV)

Oh, sweet sisters, God can and will turn your mourning to dancing. You will laugh again (Ecclesiastes 3:4 ESV). You will shout with joy again. Thank God that He is so faithful. God has given you great stamina.

Appendix

Introduction

> For nothing will be impossible with God. (Luke 1:37 ESV)

Section 1: Introduction

> Come to Me, all you who labor and are heavy laden, and I will give you rest. Take My yoke upon you and learn from Me, for I am gentle and lowly in heart, and you will find rest for your souls. (Matthew 11:28–29 NIV)

Day 1:

> Be gracious to me, O Lord, for I am in distress; my eye is wasted from grief; my soul and my body also. For my life is spent with sorrow, and my years with sighing; my strength fails because of my iniquity, and my bones waste away. (Psalm 31:9–10 ESV)

> How long, LORD? Will you forget me forever? How long will you hide your face from me? How long must I wrestle with my thoughts and day after day have sorrow in my heart? How long will my enemy triumph over me? Look on me and answer, LORD my God. Give light to my eyes, or I will sleep in death, and my enemy will say, "I have overcome him, "and my foes will rejoice when I fall. But I trust in your unfailing love; my heart rejoices in your salvation I will sing the LORD's praise, for he has been good to me. (Psalm 13 NIV)

Day 2:

> My God, my God, why have you forsaken me? Why are you so far from saving me, from the words of my

groaning? O my God, I cry by day, but you do not answer, and by night, but I find no rest. (Psalm 22:1–2 ESV)

Listen to my words, Lord, consider my lament. Hear my cry for help, my King and my God, for to you I pray. In the morning, Lord, you hear my voice; in the morning I lay my requests before you and wait expectantly. (Psalm 5:1–3 NIV)

Day 3:

Come to Me, all you who labor and are heavy laden, and I will give you rest. Take My yoke upon you and learn from Me, for I am gentle and lowly in heart, and you will find rest for your souls. (Matthew 11:28–29 NIV)

"Father, if you are willing, remove this cup from me. Nevertheless, not my will, but yours, be done." (Luke 22:42 ESV)

Day 4:

The Lord is close to the brokenhearted and saves those who are crushed in spirit. (Psalm 34:18 NIV)

You have kept count of my tossings; put my tears in your bottle. Are they not in your book? (Psalm 56:8 ESV)

The Lord himself goes before you and will be with you; he will never leave you nor forsake you. Do not be afraid; do not be discouraged. (Deuteronomy 31:8 NIV)

Day 5:

Though you have made me see troubles, many and bitter, you will restore my life again; from the depths of the earth, you will again bring me up. You will increase my honor and comfort me once more. (Psalm 71:20–21 NIV)

And the peace of God, which surpasses all understanding, will guard your hearts and your minds in Christ Jesus. (Philippians 4:7 ESV)

If any of you lacks wisdom, you should ask God, who gives generously to all without finding fault, and it will be given to you. (James 1:5 NIV)

He will cover you with his feathers. He will shelter you with his wings. His faithful promises are your armor and protection. (Psalm 91:4 NLT)

Section 2: Introduction

But you, Lord, are a compassionate and gracious God, slow to anger, abounding in love and faithfulness. (Psalm 86:15 NIV)

Day 6:

May your unfailing love come to me, Lord, your salvation, according to your promise. (Psalm 119:41 NIV)

For this is how God loved the world: He gave his one and only Son, so that everyone who believes in him will not perish but have eternal life. (John 3:16 NLT)

The LORD appeared to him from far away. I have loved you with an everlasting love; therefore have continued my faithfulness to you. (Jeremiah 31:3 ESV)

See what great love the Father has lavished on us, that we should be called children of God! And that is what we are!

The reason the world does not know us is that it did not know him. (1 John 3:1 NIV)

No, in all these things we are more than conquerors through him who loved us. For I am convinced that neither death nor life, neither angels nor demons, neither the present nor the future, nor any powers, neither height nor depth, nor anything else in all creation, will be able to separate us from the love of God that is in Christ Jesus our Lord. (Romans 8:37–39 NIV)

Day 7:

You then, my child, be strengthened by the grace that is in Christ Jesus. (2 Timothy 2:1 ESV)

Three times I pleaded with the Lord to take it away from me. But he said to me, "My grace is sufficient for you, for my power is made perfect in weakness." Therefore, I will boast all the more gladly about my weaknesses, so that Christ's power may rest on me. (2 Corinthians 12:8–9 NIV)

Day 8:

For You, Lord, are good, and ready to forgive, And abundant in mercy to all those who call upon You. (Psalm 86:5 NKJV)

The thief comes only to steal and kill and destroy. I came that they may have life and have it abundantly. (John 10:10 ESV)

The steadfast love of the Lord never ceases; his mercies never come to an end, they are new every morning; great is your faithfulness. (Lamentations 3:22–23 ESV)

But if you do not forgive others their trespasses, neither will your Father forgive your trespasses. (Matthew 6:15 ESV)

Day 9:

But you, Lord, are a compassionate and gracious God, slow to anger, abounding in love and faithfulness. (Psalm 86:15 NIV)

Jesus called his disciples to him and said, "I have compassion for these people; they have already been with me three days and have nothing to eat. I do not want to send them away hungry, or they may collapse on the way." His disciples answered, "Where could we get enough bread in this remote place to feed such a crowd?" "How many loaves do you have?" Jesus asked. "Seven," they replied, "and a few small fish." He told the crowd to sit down on the ground. Then he took the seven loaves and the fish, and when he had given thanks, he broke them and gave them to the disciples, and they in turn to the people. They all ate and were satisfied. Afterward the disciples picked up seven basketfuls of broken pieces that were left over. The number of those who ate was four thousand men, besides women and children. (Matthew 15:32–38 NIV)

Day 10:

For the word of the Lord is right and true; he is faithful in all he does. (Psalm 33:4 NIV)

The Lord himself goes before you and will be with you he will never leave you nor forsake you. Do not be afraid; do not be discouraged. (Deuteronomy 31:8 NIV)

Section 3: Introduction

> My soul clings to the dust; Revive me according to Your word. (Psalm 119:25 NKJV)

Day 11:

> For you formed my inward parts; you knitted me together in my mother's womb. I praise you, for I am fearfully and wonderfully made. Wonderful are your works my soul knows it very well. (Psalm 139:13-14 ESV)
>
> For I know the plans I have for you, declares the LORD, plans for welfare and not for evil, to give you a future and a hope. (Jeremiah 29:11 ESV)
>
> See what great love the Father has lavished on us, that we should be called children of God! And that is what we are! The reason the world does not know us is that it did not know him. (1 John 3:1 NIV)
>
> For we are God's handiwork, created in Christ Jesus to do good works, which God prepared in advance for us to do. (Ephesians 2:10 NIV)
>
> Finally, be strong in the Lord and in the strength of his might. (Ephesians 6:10 ESV)
>
> Keep me as the apple of your eye; hide me in the shadow of your wings. (Psalm 17:8 ESV)
>
> I can do all things through Christ who strengthens me. (Philippians 4:13 NKJV)
>
> Look at the birds of the air; they do not sow or reap or store away in barns, and yet your heavenly Father

feeds them. Are you not much more valuable than they? (Matthew 6:26 NIV)

The Lord will fulfill his purpose for me; your steadfast love, O Lord, endures forever. Do not forsake the work of your hands. (Psalm 138:8 ESV)

For the Lord your God is living among you. He is a mighty savior. He will take delight in you with gladness. With his love, he will calm all your fears. He will rejoice over you with joyful songs. (Zephaniah 3:17 NLT)

Day 12:

For he satisfies the longing soul, and the hungry soul he fills with good things. (Psalm 107:9 ESV)

And I will give you a new heart, and a new spirit I will put within you. And I will remove the heart of stone from your flesh and give you a heart of flesh. (Ezekiel 36:26 ESV)

Day 13:

Don't copy the behavior and customs of this world, but let God transform you into a new person by changing the way you think. Then you will learn to know God's will for you, which is good and pleasing and perfect. (Romans 12:2 NLT)

Day 14:

What shall we say to these things? If God is for us, who can be against us? (Romans 8:31 ESV)

Even if my father and mother abandon me, the Lord will hold me close. (Psalm 27:10 NLT)

He came into the very world he created, but the world didn't recognize him. He came to his own people, and even they rejected him. (John 1:10–11 NLT)

Day 15:

Do not be anxious about anything, but in every situation, by prayer and petition, with thanksgiving, present your requests to God. [7]And the peace of God, which transcends all understanding, will guard your hearts and your minds in Christ Jesus. (Philippians 4:6–7 NIV)

Give all your worries and cares to God, for he cares about you. (1 Peter 5:7 NLT)

Section 4: Introduction

And after you have suffered a little while, the God of all grace, who has called you to his eternal glory in Christ, will himself restore, confirm, strengthen, and establish you. (1 Peter 5:10 ESV)

Day 16:

Hope deferred makes the heart sick, but a desire fulfilled is a tree of life. (Proverbs 13:12 ESV)

No one who hopes in you will ever be put to shame, but shame will come on those who are treacherous without cause. (Psalm 25:3 NIV)

May the God of hope fill you with all joy and peace as you trust in him, so that you may overflow with hope by the power of the Holy Spirit. (Romans 15:13 NIV)

For whatever was written in former days was written for our instruction, that through endurance and through the encouragement of the Scriptures we might have hope. (Romans 15:4 ESV)

Day 17:

Now faith is confidence in what we hope for and assurance about what we do not see. (Hebrews 11:1 NIV)

Pray continually, give thanks in all circumstances; for this is God's will for you in Christ Jesus. (1 Thessalonians 5:17–18 NIV)

Keep this Book of the Law always on your lips; meditate on it day and night, so that you may be careful to do everything written in it. Then you will be prosperous and successful. (Joshua 1:8 NIV)

I will remember the deeds of the LORD; yes, I will remember your miracles of long ago. (Psalm 77:11 NIV)

Day 18:

May the God of hope fill you with all joy and peace as you trust in him, so that you may overflow with hope by the power of the Holy Spirit. (Romans 15:13 NIV)

Day 19:

Trust in the Lord with all your heart, and do not lean on your own understanding. In all your ways acknowledge him, and he will make straight your paths. (Proverbs 3:5–6 ESV)

Day 20:

I can do all things through Christ who strengthens me. (Philippians 4:13 NKJV)

For nothing will be impossible with God. (Luke 1:37 ESV)

Remember not the former things, nor consider the things of old. Behold, I am doing a new thing; now it springs forth, do you not perceive it? I will make a way in the wilderness and rivers in the desert. (Isaiah 43:18–19 ESV)

Conclusion:

She is clothed with strength and dignity; she can laugh at the days to come. She speaks with wisdom, and faithful instruction is on her tongue. (Proverbs 31:25–26 NIV)

The light shines in the darkness, and the darkness has not overcome it. (John 1:5 ESV)

But those who hope in the LORD will renew their strength. They will soar on wings like eagles; they will run and not grow weary; they will walk and not be faint. (Isaiah 40:31 NIV)

A time to weep, and a time to laugh; a time to mourn, and a time to dance. (Ecclesiastes 3:4 ESV)

Bibliography

Altrogge, Mark. "The Glorious Difference Between Grace and Mercy." Bible Study Tools. Posted July 8, 2021. https://www.biblestudytools.com/bible-study/topical-studies/the-glorious-life-altering-difference-between-grace-and-mercy.html.

"Everlasting." Dictionary.com. Accessed June 30, 2022, http://dictionary.reference.com/browse/everlasting.

Hazeldine, Stuart, director. *The Shack*. Lionsgate, 2017.

"Lavish." Dictionary.com. Accessed June 30, 2022. http://dictionary.reference.com/browse/lavish.

"Love." Dictionary.com. Accessed June 30, 2022. http://dictionary.reference.com/browse/love.

"Sorrow." Dictionary.com. Accessed June 30, 2022. https://www.dictionary.com/browse/sorrow.

Vroegop, Mark. *Dark Clouds, Deep Mercy: Discovering the Grace of Lament*. Wheaton, IL: Crossway, 2019.

Join the community:
For more inspiration and to join the community, follow Shemeca at www.womenofendurance.com.

Instagram: womenofendurance
Facebook: womenofendurance

Printed in the United States
by Baker & Taylor Publisher Services